Ghost City

Gary Owen

Methuen Drama

Published by Methuen Drama

3 5 7 9 10 8 6 4 2

First published in 2004 by
Methuen Publishing Limited

A CIP catalogue record for this book is available from the British Library

ISBN 0 413 77437 6

Typeset by Country Setting, Kingsdown, Kent

sgriptcymru
contemporarydramawales

presents the premiere of

GHOST CITY
by Gary Owen

First performed at Chapter in Cardiff, Wales on 3 March 2004.

Note: The playscript that follows was correct at time of going to press, but may have changed during rehearsal.

CAST:

Boy and other characters	Jonathan Floyd
Mum and other characters	Nia Gwynne
Woman and other characters	Rachel Isaac
Man and other characters	Celyn Jones
Director:	Simon Harris
Designer:	Soutra Gilmour
Lighting designer:	Charles Balfour
Assistant director:	Adele Thomas
Production manager:	Stephen Hawkins
Stage manager:	Lyndsey Owen

This production is supported by:

 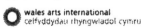

THE COMPANY
Gary Owen - WRITER

Gary's plays are *Crazy Gary's Mobile Disco* (Paines Plough and Sgript Cymru, 2001), *The Shadow of a Boy* (National Theatre, 2002), *The Drowned World* (Paines Plough, 2002), *Amser Canser* (Royal Welsh College of Music & Drama, 2003) and *Ghost City* (Sgript Cymru, 2004). *The Shadow of a Boy* was joint winner of the George Devine Award, and winner of the Meyer Whitworth Award. *The Drowned World* won a Fringe First at the Edinburgh Festival in 2002, and was joint winner of the 2003 Pearson Best Play Award. For young people he has written *The Green* for the National Theatre's Assembly project, and *SK8*, a hip-hop musical for the Theatre Royal, Plymouth.

Simon Harris - DIRECTOR

Simon Harris is Artistic Director of Sgript Cymru and Ghost City will be his fourth production for the company. Born and brought up in Swansea, Simon studied English at University College, London and trained as an actor at RADA. He founded Thin Language Theatre Company in 1992, directing *Forever Yours Marie Lou* and *Nothing to Pay* for the company, which he also adapted from the novel by Caradoc Evans. Other directorial work includes T*he Dresser* at Plymouth Theatre Royal. As a writer, his first play *Badfinger* premiered at The Donmar Warehouse and was nominated in the category for The Most Promising Playwright in the 1997 Evening Standard Drama Awards. Simon has also written *Wales>Alaska* for The Royal National Theatre Studio, *Garageland* for Steel Wasps and *Milk and Honey* for Soho Theatre Company. His previous productions for Sgript Cymru include *Franco's Bastard* by Dic Edwards, *past away* by Tracy Harris, and more recently, *Indian Country* by Meic Povey, which toured Wales and to the Traverse Theatre in Edinburgh.

Jonathan Floyd - ACTOR

Jonathan was born and raised in Bridgend, South Wales, and trained with the National Youth Theatre of Wales and at the Rose Bruford College of Speech and Drama. He made his professional debut playing the role of Nikita in Tolstoy's *The Power of Darkness* at London's Westminster Theatre. His other theatre work includes the role of Judd in John Godber's *Bouncers* which toured Bombay, Dubai, Abu Dhabi and Oman. His television work includes *Score* (BBC), *Holby City* (BBC), *Dream Team* (Sky One), Lloyd Brooke in *Doctors* (BBC) and Eddie Powell in the popular BBC period drama *Hearts of Gold*.

Celyn Jones - ACTOR

Celyn was born in Anglesey, North Wales and trained at the Manchester Youth Theatre and the Oxford School of Drama. He made his professional debut playing Henry Pratt in *Second From Last in the Sack Race* at the New Vic Theatre. His other theatre credits include Matt in *Looking for K* at the Soho Theatre, Mole in *Toad of Toad Hall* at the New Vic, Rudolph in *Cause Celebre* at the BAC, Boy in *Lear* at the Chapman Theatre, Salford, Srulik in *Ghetto* at the Library Theatre, Manchester. Ghost City will be his first production with Sgript Cymru. His film and tv credits include playing opposite Kenneth Brannagh as Blackboro in Channel 4's award winning mini-series *Shackleton*; Trevor in the BBC period drama *Hearts of Gold*; Mr Green in the children's drama *Grange Hill*; Rowan in BBC Wales' *The Bench* and Nick in *Stainless* for Mersey Film.

Nia Gwynne - ACTOR

Nia is from Neath and graduated from RADA in 1999. Her theatre work includes *Top Girls*, *Billy Liar*, and *Love Me Slender* for The New Vic Theatre. She has played Ophelia in *Who Goes There?* at The White Bear and The Evidence Room in Los Angeles, for which she was nominated as Best Supporting Actress by the L.A Weekly Theatre Awards. Her TV credits include *The Bill*, *Casualty*, *Belonging*, and *Pam fi Duw?*

Rachel Isaac - ACTOR

Rachel Isaac was born and raised in South Wales and trained at Manchester Metropolitan University School of Acting. Her first role was to play the quirky Estate Agent in Sara Sugarman's much acclaimed film *Very Annie Mary* and played Nicola in Jamie Thraives' film *The Low Down*. Theatre: Rachel appeared in Deborah Warner's multi award winning *Medea*, which toured the USA and became a smash hit on Broadway. Other theatre includes *Happy Birthday Brecht* (U. of California) for Manchester; *Camile*, *Vassa*, *The Merchant of Venice*, *Innocent as Charged* and *The Good Person of Sechuan*.
TV: Rhonda in *Murphy's Law*, Judy in *Holby City*, Trudy in *The Office* (regular, BBC and winner of two Golden Globes and 4 BAFTAS for Best Comedy). Other roles include Francesca in *I Saw You* (regular, Granada). Other BBC work includes *Man and Boy*, *Fun at the Funeral Parlour*, *The Bench*, *Tales from Pleasure Beach*, *The Secret World of Michael Fry* and *Dirty Work*.

Soutra Gilmour - DESIGNER

Theatre includes: *Antigone* (Citizens Theatre Glasgow), *Peter Pan* (The Tramway Glasgow), *The Birthday Party* (Sheffield Crucible), *The Mayor of Zalamea* (Liverpool Everyman), *Fool for Love* (English Touring Theatre), *Macbeth* (English Shakespeare Co), *Hand in Hand* (Hampstead Theatre), *Modern Dance For Beginners* (Soho Theatre), *Animal* (The Red Room), *Tear From a Glass Eye*, *Les Justes*, *Ion*, *Witness and The Flu Season* (The Gate Theatre), *Sun is Shining* (BAC Critics Choice Season), *The Women Who Swallowed a Pin*, *Winters Tale* (Southwark Playhouse), *When the World was Green* (Young Vic), *The Shadow of a Boy* (National Theatre), and *Through The Leaves* (Southwark Playhouse and Duchess Theatre). Opera credits include: *Girl of Sand* (Almeida Opera), *Everyman* (Norwich Festival), *Eight Songs for a Mad King* (World Tour), *el Cimmaron* (Queen Elizabeth Hall Southbank), *Twice Through the Heart* (Cheltenham Festival), *Bathtime* (ENO Studio), *A Better Place* (ENO, London Colesium).

Charles Balfour - LIGHTING DESIGNER

After training as an actor, Charles has designed extensively for theatre, dance and music since 1987. Theatre credits include: *Through The Leaves* (Duchess, West End), *Cake & Grace* (Jade TC, Birmingham Rep & BAC, London), *Bash* (Glasgow Citizens), *Witness* (Gate, Notting Hill), *Buster* (Theatr Clwyd), *Silent Engine & Precious Bane* (Pentabus Theatre, touring).

His many works for dance include 16 ballets with the Richard Alston Dance Company along with designs for Matthew Hawkins, Aletta Collins, Rosemary Butcher, Seven Sisters Group and Rambert.

Music/opera: *Writing to Vermeer & Hagoromo* (London Sinfonietta, Queen Elizabeth Hall, London), *Corridors* (ENO Works) *Thimble Rigging* (a collaboration with pop icon Scott Walker, QEH) and *Jordon Town* (Errollyn Wallen, Linbury Royal Opera House).

Stephen Hawkins - PRODUCTION MANAGER

Stephen graduated from the Royal Welsh College of Music and Drama with a degree in Theatre Studies and a practical training in Stage Management. He primarily works in touring theatre but also freelances for outdoor events, television and opera. Stephen first worked for Sgript Cymru in 2002 as Stage Manager for Tracy Harris' play *past away*. More recent work includes Technical Stage Management for Theatr Y Byd's *Sex and Power at the Beau Rivage*, Stage Technician and flyman for an international tour of Param Vir's *Ion* with Music Theatre Wales and Stage Management of *Frida and Diego – A Love Story* by Greg Cullen for the National Youth Theatre of Wales.

Lyndsey Owen - STAGE MANAGER

Lyndsey trained in Stage Management at the Royal Welsh College of Music and Drama. Her work has continued within Wales with recent credits including *Pinocchio* at the Sherman Theatre, *Gwyneth and the Green Knight* – a children's opera, *The Electrification of The Soviet Union*, and *The Lighthouse* with Music Theatre Wales who are a contemporary opera company. She has also worked and toured with Clwyd Theatr Cymru on *To Kill a Mockingbird* and *Oh What a Lovely War*. This is Lyndsey's first production with Sgript Cymru.

Adele Thomas - ASSISTANT DIRECTOR

Adele graduated from Cambridge University in 2003 where she worked as director on a number of projects including Shakespeare's *Coriolanus* and *A Midsummer Night's Dream*, Edward Bond's *Passion and Bingo*. She is interested in new writing and has been involved twice with Cambridge's new writing festival Smorgasbord, as well as premiering a new work by young writers in the Swansea Grand Theatre's Arts wing. She also organises mixed media events and is involved in a Cardiff based avant garde music night The Quarter as well as being a DJ herself.

sgriptcymru
contemporarydramawales

sgriptcymru is the national company for contemporary drama in Wales, specialising in new writing by Welsh and Wales-based playwrights.

The company holds a pivotal role in discovering and promoting exciting new voices for the stage. Unique in its exclusive dedication to producing new writing in both Welsh and English, **sgript**cymru is also a development organisation that works with emerging playwrights at the grassroots level, as well as a commissioning company working with professional playwrights offering valuable freedom to their creativity and placing their vision at the heart of its work.

Through **sgript**cymru's professional support to dramatists and its award-winning programme of new productions each year, the company aims to ensure the continuing existence of a new writing culture in Wales and to enhance its place in the wider world. The company has gained an enviable reputation for the quality and range of its work in theatres nationwide since it's inception in 2000.

"The excellent new writing company," *The Guardian, June 2003*

"...testament to the strength of writing in Wales and the vision of Sgript Cymru," *The Big Issue Cymru, May 2001*

sgriptcymru - productions:

- *Yr Hen Blant* by Meic Povey (2000)
- *Art and Guff* by Catherine Tregenna (in association with Soho Theatre Co.) (2001)
- *Crazy Gary's Mobile Disco* by Gary Owen (co –production with Paines Plough) (2001)
- *Mab* by Sera Moore-Williams (co-production with Y Gymraes) (2001)
- *Ysbryd Beca* by Geraint Lewis (2001)
- *Franco's Bastard* by Dic Edwards (2002)
- *Dosbarth* by Geraint Lewis (2002)
- *past away* by Tracy Harris (2002)
- *Diwrnod Dwynwen* by Fflur Dafydd, Angharad Devonald, Angharad Elen, Meleri Wyn James, Dafydd Llewelyn and Nia Roberts (2003)
- *Indian Country* by Meic Povey (2003)
- *Amdani!* by Bethan Gwanas (2003)

sgriptcymru - awards:

- *Crazy Gary's Mobile Disco* by Gary Owen (Best New Writing Award in the inaugural Theatre in Wales Awards 2001)
- *Franco's Bastard* by Dic Edwards (Best New Writing Award in the Theatre in Wales Awards 2002)
- Eiry Thomas as Gwyneth in *Indian Country* by Meic Povey (Best Actress in the Theatre in Wales Awards 2003)
- Sion Pritchard as Young Mos in *Indian Country* by Meic Povey (Most Promising Performer in the Theatre in Wales Awards 2003)
- Director Elen Bowman for *Amdani!* by Bethan Gwanas (Best Welsh Language Production in the Theatre in Wales Awards 2003)

sgriptcymru - company:

Artistic Director:	Simon Harris
Administrative Director:	Mai Jones
Associate Director:	Elen Bowman
Literary Manager:	Angharad Elen
Marketing Manager:	Siân Melangell Dafydd
Administrative Officer:	Meleri Thomas

Artistic Associate:	Bethan Jones
Associate Writer:	Meic Povey

sgriptcymru - Board of Directors:

Ann Beynon (chair)
Frances Medley (vice chair)
Philippa Davies
Iestyn George
Nicola Heywood-Thomas
Richard Houdmont
Elwyn Tudno Jones
David Seligman
Lucy Shorrocks
Elinor Williams
Mared Hughes (associate member).

sgriptcymru - contact

If you would like to be on the Sgript Cymru free mailing list please send your details to:
sgriptcymru
Chapter
Market Road
Canton
Cardiff
CF5 1QE

T: 029 2023 6650
E: sgriptcymru@sgriptcymru.com
www.sgriptcymru.com
sgriptcymru is a registered charity no: 702117

GHOST CITY

CARDIFF: Chapter Arts Centre
3 – 20 March 8 pm
Tickets: 029 2030 4400

MILFORD HAVEN: Torch Theatre
Tues. 23rd and Wed. 24th March 7.30 pm
Tickets: 01646 695267

ABERYSTWYTH: Aberystwyth Arts Centre
Fri. 26th and Sat. 27th March 7.30 pm
Tickets: 01970 623232

MOLD: Clwyd Theatre Cymru
Fri. 2nd and Sat. 3rd April 7.45 pm
Tickets: 0845 330 3565

PLYMOUTH: Theatre Royal
11 – 15 May
Tickets: 01752 267 222

BRADFORD: Theatre in the Mill
21 + 22 May
Tickets: 01274 233200 or theatre@bradford.ac.uk

BIRMINGHAM: The Door, Birmingham Rep.
25 + 26 May
Tickets: 01212364455

LUTON: The Hat Factory
27 + 28 May
Tickets: 0121 236 4455

NEW YORK, USA: 59e59 Theaters
1 June – 13 June
Tickets: 212-279-4200 or www.ticketcentral.com

LONDON: Arcola
17 June – 10 July (excluding Sundays)
Tickets: 020 7503 1646

For Jimmy Owen

Acknowledgements

Thanks to Sgript Cymru. Thanks to Michael McCoy and
Josh Varney. Thanks to Rollo Carpenter for creating Jabberwacky (with which you can chat at www.jabberwacky.com).
Thanks to Jody Zellen for creating ghostcity.com. And
thanks to Cardiff: thanks for talking so loud that I could not
help but overhear; thanks for whispering so quietly I just had
to find out what you were saying; thanks for leaving your
post conveniently open on the kitchen table; thanks for
phoning in; thanks for playing my tune; thanks for explaining
in simple language just what the problem with me is; thanks
for all your memories; thanks to the museum guides, and
record-keepers, and librarians: and thank you, thank you,
thank you, to those of you who have given me a home.

Ghost City

25   The Station for the Nation

Llantrisant Road, 0600.

>It's six a.m. precisely
>And a balmy five degrees here
>In the capital
>– doubtless somewhat cooler, and wetter, and worse
>For you poor sods up north –
>And this is Glyn Daniels coming
>Live and direct via radio waves
>On ninety-three to one-oh-four,
>The station . . . for the nation.

Beat.

>I've just been told I –

Beat.

>I'd like to apologise for my use of the word 's-o-d-s'
>>in that last link.
>I'd like it to be known that in using the word 's-o-d-s'
>>in that last link
>I did not mean to imply that the inhabitants of North
>>Wales are
>Clods of earth.
>Or enthusiastic practisers of buggery.

Beat.

>Have you cut me off?
>Have you fucking cut me off, you jumped-up little –

Beat.

>Now you fucking listen.
>I have served on this station
>– and I use that word advisedly, 'served' as in 'time' –
>For seventeen bastard years
>And I've tussled with little shits like you before
>And let me tell you when Glyn Daniels tussles with
>>a shit

It's invariably the shit that ends up flushed down the
    bog hole, alright?

Beat.

Actually I do know who your fucking dad is.
And more than that, I know who, in this office,
Your fucking dad is fucking.
Ah. Yes.
Weren't expecting that, were you.

Beat.

Sorry about that, ladies and gents.
Just where my producer usually sits
This morning I find a . . . young thing
Has slipped in on a six-week contract
And this young thing is of the opinion I might have
Offended some of the great Welsh listenership
With my use of the word 's-o-d'.
This young thing thinks it knows the Glyn Daniels
    audience
Better than Glyn Daniels does.
So let's see, shall we.
Let's have a little listen and see.
You can phone, you can fax, you can email, you can
    text.
Let the Glynster know if you've been shocked from
    your skins
By my use of the word –
– I won't say it again.
There's no need to be gratuitous, is there.
In the meantime – Sheena Easton, with 'Nine to Five'.
Oh fuck yeah. Your fucking dad.
Fucking in that he's a fucking clueless tosser.
And fucking in that he's been fucking his way round
    this building
Like a tomcat on –

He experiences a sudden, unexpected pain.

He wasn't always that way.

He used to have a clue.
More than a clue.
He used –
– before you were born –
He used to be –
He was a broadcaster.
Simple as that.
A broadcaster.
He cast his words into the ether and
The nation listened, broadly.
And now –
– Sheena Easton there, a lovely little girl
And a Celt to boot, of course.
So let's head to the phones and find out just how
   lily-livered you are.
Line one, we've got –

Beat.

Line two.
Line –
Okay. There seems to be
A little problem with the phones this morning.
We'll try the email.

Beat.

There also seems to be
A problem with the email this morning.

Beat.

We'll try the phones again.
Gwyneth in East Williamston, you up yet?
Roger in Pembrey?
Wendy in Tregaron?
Anybody?

Beat.

Come on.

Beat.

Just – pick up the phone.
You don't have to come on the air.
Just call in.
You know the number.
If you're there –
– and you are, I know –
Just call in and let me hear your voice
And you don't have to say anything on the airwaves,
    just –
– I'll give you fifty quid.
Fifty quid of my own money
To the first person to call in.
You don't have to go on air.
You don't have to say a thing,
Just let me hear you breathing down the phone.
Just let me know you're alright.

24   How Does She Do It?

Romilly Road, 0751.

Finally a taxi turns up.
As Rob's getting in, he turns and says, love
– because that's my name now, 'love' –
Love, you've remembered
The electrician's coming, haven't you?
I haven't, in fact, and he knows it.
Back inside I pause
At the foot of the stairs to shout
And you better be getting up young lady,
And she shouts back
I am-uh.
Cause that's how young people talk now.
I am-uh. Leave me alone-uh.
I shout, do you want toast or cornflakes?
And she goes, can't I have Frosties-uh?
What is it – on the national curriculum?
English Language Key Stage Three –

Kids should have mastered talking like
The bloke out of what's that band –
– who are they? John Peel's favourites.
Shit.
I go back out 'cause I sort of feel I should be
Attending to the car in its moment of crisis.
I put the bonnet up and sort of stare down
At the engine.
Peer at different, specific bits of it,
In that way you do
When you're waiting for the AA man
To pitch up and pass judgement
– and then I notice. Next door.
A kid, standing.
Just standing there.
Hooded top. The hood pulled up
Over baseball cap.
And he's just watching me.
I look down at the engine,
Fiddle with the water cap and –
– I hear a thump.
This kid is standing with his back
To next door's front door
Kicking hell out of it.
The door gives way.
And the kid slips inside.
A youth has just kicked open
Next door's front door
And gone inside.
And this – in the broad light of day.

Beat.

I call the police.
Not 999, but the station on Cowbridge Road.
I say look I can't believe anyone really would,
Broad daylight first bloody thing and in full view
Of a witness, but – it did look a bit dodgy, to be honest.
The bloke says no well done
You're right to call now if you could

Keep an eye to see if anyone
Leaves the premises but please
Do not confront the intruder.
From upstairs Elen shouts,
Am you getting me those bastard Frosties or what-uh?
I shout back, darling we have no bastard Frosties
Would Kellogg's Frosties suffice, just for today?
She says, you're not funny-uh.
I say, I'm not funnier than who?
This sends her safely back into her room
So I go outside again
And stand by the car
And – wait.
The kid comes out.
Closes the door.
I look at him.
Car broke down, has it, he says.
Mmm, I say back.
He kicks the door again.
With me watching.
Kicks it open a second time and goes back in.
I'm thinking: if he comes out with a telly, I'll –
– what?
He's robbing the place in broad daylight.
He's got to have a knife at least.
The door opens
And in his hands
He's got three
Or maybe four
Digestive biscuits.
He looks at me.
He says, I'm fuck-all use with cars,
Otherwise I'd help.
That'd'be very kind of you, I say,
If you did.
He takes a bite
A big bite
Of his digestive biscuit.
Uhm . . . you don't

Actually live here, do you?
Not any more, he goes.
Me and my mum
Weren't getting on.
I live with my dad now.
I used to live here, though,
I lived here when you moved in
Which was – a year and a half ago?
I offered to help you
Carrying some plants in and you said
You were fine.

Beat.

It's alright, he goes. I know
What you must be thinking.
Young person.
Baseball cap.
You're bound to suspect, aren't you.

Beat.

I'm pouring Frosties into a bowl
When there's a knock at the door.
I open up, expecting electrician;
What I see is
Twenty-one-year-old cop.
He asks if the intruder is still in the house.
I explain that no I think it was
A false alarm; the kid, for example,
Knew we'd moved in
Just a year and a half ago.
Whereas he'd lived here for fifteen years, until
He and his mum –
The cop asks, was he carrying anything?
I say, yes. Three, or it was maybe four
Digestive biscuits.
On the other side of the road,
The electrician pulls up.
I see him start to get out,
And then he spots the cop,

And he decides to sit for a moment
Discreetly in his van.
Digestive biscuits, says the cop,
And his whole body calms down a notch.
I'm sorry for wasting your time, I go,
The cop says no no, no problem. After all:
Better safe than robbed.
Well thanks for coming so quickly, I say,
And he goes, not at all. My pleasure.
My pleasure entirely, he goes.

Beat.

When the coast is clear,
The electrician creeps out,
And wants to know the story.
I tell him – the story is,
We've got all these poncy halogen lights
And the transformers are blowing
Left, centre and right and so if you get started
I'll get some coffee on the go and
Elen thumps down the stairs
And I wonder sometimes if those stairs
Don't need looking at.
There's another knock and it's
The AA man and as I'm describing to him
Just in what exact way our car refused to start today
Elen slips out and shouts back
Thanks for the Frosties, Mum, and

She experiences a sudden, unexpected pain.

It catches me, it still does:
I still find myself thinking, Christ,
Mum, that's me now:
I am Mum, and I've got
The AA man doing the car out the front,
The electrician in the kitchen doing the lights,
Rob in a cab just about to make his train.
Elen being just fucking perfect, and
The Fall are, of course, John Peel's favourite band.

And I am getting the eye
From twenty-one-year-old cops:
I'm getting away with it.
I really fucking am.

23 Eggs and Bread

Train passing Splott Road, 0817.

Eggs and bread.
Get your eggs and bread here.
Roast albatross.
Seagull steaks.
What's that, ma'm?
A lucky black coffee?
You'd like a lucky black coffee?
I think I've got a few of those left.
Yes, I think that's the luckiest black coffee I've sold
    all morning.
There was a white coffee I sold to a gentleman
A few minutes out from Newport that might have
    been as lucky
But nothing luckier has so far this morning passed
    from my hand.
Now will you have sugar, or will you sip it as is?
A good choice: savour that bitterness,
And the rest of the day will
Seem all the more sweet.
That'll be a hundred and nineteen pence.
Oh: a two-pound coin.
A coin of two pounds.
You are a modern young lady.
I think I could accept two pounds
In place of a hundred and nineteen pence.
That might be acceptable
On condition that you see your way clear to
Favouring your trolley operative
With let's just say

Let's just call it a smile,
Could we have that?
A little hint of
Exposed tooth
To help the morning along?

He experiences a sudden and unexpected pain.

No?
Well.
Cardiff Central your next station stop, Cardiff Central.
Coming up in a hundred and eighty seconds, or
    less.
Anyone else for roast albatross?
Seagull steaks?
Eggs and bread?

22   Miss Price Returns

Willows High School, 0925.

I don't wanna come out of the cupboard, he screams
    at me.
Well that's fine, I tell him,
But why don't you come out just for now
So we can have a proper chat
And then you can go back in,
Once we're finished.
Don't wanna have a proper chat, he goes,
Just want you all to leave me alone.
Really, I say. Well that's a bit strange.
People who want to be left alone
Generally avoid attracting attention.
But people who scream and shout
And run round the place
Throwing books at other children –
Generally they're drawing attention to themselves
Because they don't want to be left alone.
He kicks against the cupboard wall six or seven times.

I wait.
Don't wanna have a proper chat with you, he goes.
Who do you want to talk to, Simon?
Wanna have a proper chat with Miss Price.

Beat.

So what do you want to talk about, I begin.
He's having none of it.
I want a proper chat with Miss Price, he screams.

Beat.

How'm I different to Miss Price? I ask.
You just are.
I look quite like her, don't I?
No you don't, he goes.
Your hair is shorter and your skin is all brown.
He's got two good points.
Three weeks in Italy have left me nicely baked,
And I got my hair cut before we went.
Fair enough, I tell him.
But if you're going to sit in that cupboard
You can't see me anyway
So it doesn't matter what I look like
It only matters how I sound.
And don't I sound like Miss Price?
No, he goes.
No? I ask him. In what way?
Don't know, he says.
You don't know?
Yes – and Miss Price always says it's alright not to
    know things
Cause learning things is why we're here.

Beat.

I never realised you were so fond of Miss Price.
He stays silent.
You've got a funny way of showing it if you are.
What d'you mean, he goes.
Well, quite a lot of the time you don't do what she asks.

Quite a lot of the time you're disruptive in her history
  class.
You swear at her several times a week to my certain
  knowledge.
And I have a sneaking suspicion it was you, Simon,
Who slashed the tyres on her car.
He doesn't answer for a while, then he goes
I wouldn't be mean to her ever again if she came back.
Well, I say, perhaps you should've taken that attitude
  earlier on.
He falls silent, and then –
– is it cause of me, he goes.
Is Miss Price gone because I was mean to her?

She experiences a sudden and unexpected pain.

Simon, course it's not your fault.
Then why can't she come back?
But she's here right now, I tell him. I mean:
I'm right here.
And he says
It's my fault, isn't it?
And there's that little tremble in the voice.
And you can hear the little kid he
Still would be, if it weren't –
– for everything.

Beat.

It's still me, Simon.
No it's not, he goes. You're Mrs Bowen. I want
  Miss Price.

Beat.

Simon. Alright.
When there's no one else around
When it's just you and me,
You can call me Miss Price.
But? he says, all smiley now, knowing he's won.
But, I want my car to remain pristine
For the rest of your school career.

Don't worry, he goes,
Anybody touches your car,
I'll fuckin kill 'em, Miss Price.

21   For Their Consideration

Westgate Street, 1019.

I'll give you a folder
We have these –
They're like these leatherette folders
Because you see your certificates
You see that one, Woodworking 2,
You see how it's all smudged and dog-eared?
It seems like a little thing;
It is a little thing.
But when you're up there in front of them
They've got five, ten minutes to make a decision
And so they're looking for little things.
They're searching for clues
That are gonna tip them one way
Or the other.

Beat.

No, you're right, maybe the magistrates
Themselves won't actually look through your certificates
But somebody will.
There'll be a case worker who will,
And they'll have another dozen cases to work that
    morning
So the point is the same:
They're on the lookout for short cuts.
Their eyes are peeled wide for what
At the poker table we call 'tells'.
So this folder. It has leatherette covers and
Plastic envelopes inside.
You put your certificates in them and they look
Smart. Respectable. Decent.

Beat.

> There's one other thing.
> And I don't know how you feel about this.
> And that's your Christianity.
> Now, I'm not sure –

Stops.

> The key here is understatement.
> If you wanna use it,
> The key is not to say too much.
> Don't say to them, I've become a Christian
> And it's changed my life completely
> Cause it's obviously not done.
> I mean, I don't wanna sound like too much
> Of an atheist about this
> But it's obviously not changed your life
> Completely, has it? I can smell that on your breath.

He experiences a sudden, unexpected pain.

> You see lots of kids
> Who're going up before the magistrates
> They . . . discover that they've found a friend in
>   the Lord.
> Well I advise them strongly against mentioning it at all
> And I never mention it myself.
> So. If I say something with you,
> That might count for a bit.
> They might prick up their ears and go
> That old git Williams, he never
> Usually lays this God crap on us
> So what's going on here?

Beat.

> It's not gonna count for much.
> But if I say you've become a churchgoer
> And the magistrate believes me
> Then he's gonna know:
> That's a moral code

You've committed to live by.
And at least he's gonna have that
In the back of his mind.

Beat.

I never, ever say that sort of thing.
But I will with you,
Because with you it's genuine,
Isn't it?

20   Learning to Fall

Sophia Gardens, 1102.

After some little practice
In the proper method of walking,
Having thereby attained some knowledge
Of the art of balance,
The student should make up his mind
To learn to fall correctly.
No amount of theoretical knowledge
Will enable a student to accomplish this.
Actual practice is
Absolutely necessary.

Beat.

In order to fall without injury
The student must make injury
The very least of his worries.
He must occupy himself entirely
With the fact of having been thrown;
Of having lost the bout.
The anguish of loss,
Of physical and psychic defeat,
Is expressed in a sharp slamming of the arm
Against the mat, which should occur a fraction of
    a second
Before the body hits the ground.

Observing this expression of anguish-in-defeat
The universe finds itself unable to inflict
The further punishment
Of physical pain.
On witnessing the absolute defeat of person and spirit
The universe finds physical pain
A trivial and brute means of instruction
Which it then refrains from employing.
Therefore on all occasions
When you are thrown
You must express your defeat in the face of the universe
With this sharp slapping of the mat.
As hard as you can.
The harder you slap, the less pain you will then feel –

She experiences a sudden, unexpected pain.

It is said that in the dusty yellow mornings that follow
Great catastrophes
Only those whose minds are destroyed feel physical
pain.
Those whose minds are intact
Wander the ruins in perfect silence
And contemplate the scale of the crime committed
against them.
The universe perceives that at this stage
To inflict mere physical pain would be crass:
A distraction from the true horror.
It is only when horror does its job
And these bewildered minds finally crack
That the universe resorts to blunter tools.

Beat.

It is wise to begin practice of the first break-fall
From a sitting position, on the ground.

19   Families Need Fathers

Queen's Street, 1142.

Unaccustomed as I am to public speaking.

Beat.

You know I thought people who spoke on the public
  streets
Were just nutters, I gotta be honest with you.
Well, wack-wack-oops.
I was wrong about that, wasn't I.
Cause here I am today and I'm hardly –
Look, if just one or two of you could stop
This won't take ever so long.
I appreciate you're all
Going places.
But if any of you
Look at yourselves and say,
Ah yes, my dad, he contributed, he put in
To the person I am today,
This person who is headed places,
Then I think you owe it to your dad
To stop and listen.

Beat.

Well if that doesn't strike a nerve –
I have to say I can't quite believe none of you
Feel you owe your dads a damn thing –

Beat.

Right, fair enough, the other way round then.
If any of you –
I don't wanna be prejudiced about this
But if you find kids take the piss out of you on the
  street,
Or waiters never seem to notice you,
Or everyone who's your boss is a bum-fluffed teenager:

And you realise now that it's not cause you're
Intrinsically a nancy, it's cause you never had
A clear male parental input
Then don't you owe it to yourself
To stop
And do what you can?

Beat.

Thank you.

Beat.

Unaccustomed as I . . .

He stops.

Families need fathers.
It's – that simple.
We are needed as providers of sperm.
I don't mean to be – graphic
But, we are. There it is.
We are needed as providers of cash
– Now, come on: you can't argue with that.
But I'm not on about those needs.
I'm on about –
There are child psychologists,
Lady child psychologists,
Who identify the father-figure
As playing a vital role in forcing the infant
To progress beyond the child-mother pair bond.
In encouraging it to recognise the limits and needs
    of other persons.
Cause, as we know, mothers all too often suppress
    their own needs
In order to attend to the needs of their children.
These lady psychologists say
The father plays a vital role in preparing the infant
For interaction with the hard, cold objective world.
A world that you often can only get through
With a raised voice, or a stamped foot, or a very hard,
Very definite kind of stare.

A world in which your team loses and loses and loses
   again
No matter how loud you sing and scream and chant;
A world in which the fragile, beautiful miracle of love
Finds expression through sex, which is all
Belchings and heavings and smells.

Beat.

Families need fathers.
They need them to learn from.
They need them to practise on.
Families need fathers.

He experiences a sudden, unexpected pain.

And fathers need families.
If we can't channel our energies
Positively
Creatively
Into the family
Then where will our energies be discharged?
Then what will our energies become?

Beat.

Thank you all very much for your attention.
I know you're very busy.

18   Warranty Extension

Queen's Street, 1158.

Because maybe
You have a son or a daughter you could pass this
   product on to.
Maybe
You have a spouse or life partner
You could pass this product on to.
Maybe you have a girl-
Or boy-friend who would benefit from its functionality.

Maybe on the day
You decide you're done with this product's sleek chrome
And matt blackness you'll wake –
With a 'casual' at your side,
Ruffling up the bedclothes,
Sweating gently into your linen.
You could pass the product on to her
Or him
In lieu of cab fare.
They could ride home with it cradled in their arms –
Oh, no sir. Five hundred pounds is a trifling sum
To spend on warranty extension.
You've already committed to purchasing the product
You've already admitted you need the product in
    your life,
So – another five hundred pounds
To ensure the product's functionality will continue
    uninterrupted?
Five hundred pounds? For three long years
Of smooth, hassle-free, dependable functionality?
And you need something you can depend on:

She experiences a sudden, unexpected pain.

You, more than anyone I've seen all week.
Five hundred, hundred pence to ensure
Our fully-clued up service crews are available to you
Twenty-five seven.
So that in the unlikely event of product let-down
You need only call and quote your post code –
And our fully tooled-up service crews will
Express their way
Jet pack their way
Ride and drive and hijack
Their way to your door
And with an application of elbow juice and sonic
    screwdriving and
Good old fashioned Britannic ultra-violence
They will beat – literally –
Your product back into working order.

Restoring the flow of info-tainment to your home.
Or flat.
Or bed-sitting room.

Beat.

You're sold.
I think you are.
And now if sir will make his way? Thank you.
I should mention now,
This model supplies sans the benefit of a SCART cable
Which is absolutely vital to the product's functionality.
You'll be wanting one of those, then, and
That'll be another seven quid.

17   They Should All Get Back to Palestine

Havelock Street, 1220.

Hi. Hello.
Could I speak to uhh
Ms Nancy Regan, please.
Oh that's you
Mrs Regan.
Mrs Regan of Pooles Lane, London?
No I'm not trying to sell you anything, honestly –
I'm calling about a letter
Which I believe you wrote to the *Western Mail*
Some days ago.
Yes, we are thinking of publication, it's just that
    occasionally
Jokers, losers and muppets
Like to write in to newspapers under assumed names.
So I am phoning just to make sure
You wrote these words and intend them for the public
    eye.

Beat.

Yes I'm sure you do write a lot of letters.

I can imagine that to be the case about you.
Perhaps if I quote, you'll recall this specific one.
'Dear Sir', you open
– which is a very classy salutation
For the editor of a mere provincial –
As a visitor to Cardiff on Saturday April 27.
I was appalled and amazed to hear and see
A march of Palestinian Jihad supporters
Extolling the extinction of USA, UK, President Bush, etc.
These are your words?
You recognise them now?
Do you recall also that you continued:
We as taxpayers are paying the police to protect
Those who want to bring down our country
(But are happy to live off our benefits).
If they feel that strongly about exterminating Israel
Then they should return to Palestine.
Those were your words
Weren't they, Nancy?

Beat.

Yes.
Uh-huh.
Yes, that's right, you did go on at
Much greater length there in the middle
But we reserve the right to edit for the sake of brevity.
Well, we say brevity, we mean
For the sake of our sanity.

Beat.

No, I'm sure you haven't been spoken to this way
By a sub-editor before,
You sour-blooded, shrivel-titted cunt.

Beat.

Are you still there?
Are you – fucking hell – speechless?
Well that suits me. I have a certain amount to say
Which will fill the gap admirably.

Guess what, Nancy. Nance.
I am not really
A *Western Mail* sub-editor.
I am an enforcer.
For an anarcho-syndicalist
Neo-Luddite
Post-nationalist
Extreme hip-hop collective.
And we are fucking sick
Of you English fuckers
Dumping your toxic waste onto us.
Case in point, that Nick Griffin twat,
You exported him to our once peacefully multicultural
    land,
And now he's trying to ethnically scour Powys and
    turn it into
Lebensraum for sexually inadequate white boys.
Well, don't fucking worry.
We've got that cunt's number.
And now we've got your number too, Nancy.

He experiences a sudden, unexpected pain.

She puts down the phone.
And frankly I'm glad.
Hannah's off sick this week so I've been left with
The arts pages to do all by my fucking self.
I've said to Neil, I can't be doing letters and arts
In the same fucking week.
A man's only got so much fucking bile, for Christ's sake.
Does he listen?
Does he fuck.

16   You Are Now Leaving the Galactic Habitable Zone

Techniquest, 1255.

And so you've got to ask yourself – why
This rush of sensation and experience?

What's it all about?

Cause think: the centre of the galaxy is just black
    holes and

Neutron stars bumping off each other and with

All that gamma radiation, nothing can live there.

So first your star's got to be on the fringes, in the
    habitable zone.

And then your planet's got to form at the right
    distance from the sun

So it will neither bake nor freeze.

And what are the chances of that? Not fucking good.

And then further out in the system

There has to be a big gas giant

At just the right orbit to sweep up the rubble

From the solar accretion disc.

Beat.

Oh God . . . yes, I think this is all relevant, actually

You've asked me a specific question

And so I'm trying to establish some general principles

From which I can derive a specific answer – alright?

And it doesn't

Fucking

Help

Having you fuckin looking at your watch every five
    seconds.

Alright.

I've forgotten where I was now.

Okay.

You need a magnetic field to ward off cosmic rays,

An ozone layer to soak up the ultraviolet.

You might get one or the other, but getting them both?

Not bloody likely. But tough. Both is what you need.

Then you need primitive single-celled life to emerge;

You've got to be jammy enough to pull that one off,

But it turns out the real bugger is getting the single-
    celled fuckers

To move beyond their primeval simplicity.

You need some sort of minor cataclysm

Which doesn't fuck the planet completely, but shakes
     things up
And gets evolution going, and then
Millions of years later
You get us.
So – do you see?
Do you see – how unlikely it is?
Try and like hold it in your head –
– all those impossible things that have to happen
And they ALL have to come right
For us to even be born.
Try and focus it all, in your mind.
Are you focusing it?
Are you?

Beat.

I don't think you are.
Not really.
Cause if you are –
– then how come you don't wanna go back out
     with me?

Beat.

It's obvious how it works.
Oh my God I swear you are the most unimaginative
     cunt
Ever to walk the face of the earth.
Everyone. Everyone who understands
Just how fuckin unlikely it is that we are here at all,
It ends up fuckin their head.
No one
Thinks about this stuff and then
Shrugs
And scratches their arse
And goes, I don't see what difference it makes.

Beat.

As you in fact have just done.

Beat.

>I can't believe I'm acting like this.
>I am cooler than this.
>I am much cooler than you.
>Oh fuck no no I didn't mean – don't go yet
>Just fucking TWO minutes more, please.
>Please.

Beat.

>Thank you.
>What I'm getting at is
>It's so unlikely that we're here at all
>It either means a God created us
>Or, it means that we are the most important thing in
>In a billion, billion universes.
>Either way we are a fuckin miracle.
>And I don't believe miracles happen for nothing
>I believe we are here for a reason.
>I believe the reason we are here
>Is love.

A pause.

>I knew you'd laugh
>When I said that.
>It's alright, I'm not upset:
>I'd been preparing myself.
>No, don't worry. I know you're fed up with me.
>I know cause I went round to your flat
>And you've changed the fucking locks, haven't you?
>I mean if you'd asked
>I would've just
>Given the key back.
>Locksmiths are expensive, for fuck's sake, there was –

Beat.

>– you see
>I actually think all this happened and we met
>Because we were meant to love each other.
>Don't you fucking

Beat.

Laugh at me.

She experiences a sudden, unexpected pain.

Do you ever wonder why
None of your exes speak to you now?
You can't see a pattern there, at all?
No?
No, course you can't.
What really pisses me off is
You're gonna tell people
You've done your best to be kind
And reasonable, and fair,
And you'll get a bit teary-eyed as you say it
And everyone will fucking believe you.
When what you've actually done is
You've switched off your phone
And changed the locks
And gone and hidden at your mum's,
So I can't bother you. Or stress you out.
Or emotionally exhaust you any more than I –
– you know walking over here I saw
A kid sat on a bench.
He had this little dog on his lap
He was holding his arms around its body
And pressing his cheek up against its face
Holding it really tight
For warmth, I expect
But also, out of love.
His face was –

Beat.

I couldn't believe we were all walking past him.
I couldn't believe I was.
He looked me right in the eye
And I walked past him
And I knew he needed someone
And I – am someone.

In spite of everything you say. I am.
But still I walked past. Cause I was coming to see you.
He could die tonight.
He might well,
Cause who's gonna save him, but for me?
And so what I'm saying is
Please don't let me be
Wasting my time on you.
Just – say we can meet for a drink.
Just as friends.
Say that, and I'll go.
And then you can get back to your desk
And get on with your
Oh so fucking important job.

15   Preparedness and Resilience

Television broadcast intercepted at the Temple of Peace, 1305.

I've pondered long and hard over this speech.
'Speech'.
As if that were
As if a speech could be adequate for such a grave
    circumstance.

Beat.

My colleagues and I
Have not been sleeping well for some time now.
Many of you
Will have been sleeping untroubled.
Sleeping like babies.
'Sleeping the sleep of the just.'
And that's entirely as it should be.
You have the business of life to be getting on with
My colleagues and I,
We have little to distract us
From the matter in hand.
Our day-to-day needs are taken care of

Leaving us free to read and compose
Briefings, memoranda, position papers.
It's some time since I composed any kind of briefing,
    of course.
Nowadays, I am invariably composed towards.

Beat.

In considering what to say to you, today,
All these varieties of information and opinion
Have proven
Ultimately
Unhelpful.

Beat.

That is not what I wanted to –

Beat.

I find myself recalling an incident.
This was a few years ago and
I was a comparatively junior member of the
    administration.
My security detail was – comparatively light.
I was able to evade surveillance
And sneak off for a walk with my son.
The simplest thing, but impossible for me now, of
    course.
I had to carry him most of the time
But there were brief intervals in which he was
Entirely self-propelled
And on one of his rushing solo excursions
My son approached –
– a tramp, collapsed and abandoned on the street.
He walked up to
This – gentleman
With no fear in his eyes
Not a hint of trepidation
Just an – amiable curiosity.
He even reached out to touch the man.
I recognised the gesture,

It was the same movement my son used for stroking
  our cat.
I had to say, no, Harry.
No.
You don't touch.
He looked round at me, his look asking – why?
And by way of explanation, I found myself saying
No, Harry. Dirty. You don't touch.
And he –
– accepted that.
He accepted that entirely.
He took a step back and
His face now closed and careful
He looked up and down the drunk,
Then turned away, turned on his heels
And walked back to me.

Beat.

What I need now
Is your trust.
And that's a huge thing to ask for.
My position
My judgement on these matters
Is complete and coherent.
I cannot at this time explain fully why
As such revelation would endanger
Our agents in the field.
And so.
I'm going to say nothing
To attempt to justify
What everyone knows we have to do.
I will say nothing
I could be called to account on.
I will simply ask you to trust me.
I feel I can ask that.
I feel you do trust me.
After all, many of you
Sleep at night.
I am . . . not so blessed

In that regard.
And I believe you sleep because – you trust me.

He experiences a sudden, unexpected pain.

You must.
Or surely – you would get up now
You would rise up and
You would do
Whatever it took to stop me.

14   This is Fuckin Cardiff

Gorsedd Gardens, 1358.

What's he saying?
What?
He's saying – that's the what?
He's saying that's the City Hall.
He's saying that's the City Hall like the Town Hall
   in Milford?
Well that's bollocks.
That's nothing like the Town Hall in Milford.
That thing's all big and grey and it's got lions and shit
And the Town Hall in Milford it's
Like a fuckin Portakabin isn't it.
The fuckin twat. Talking bollocks like that.
What's he saying now?
Whassat sir?
Don't let what?
– Jesus Christ look at the fuckin speed on that
   ambulance.
Fuckin hell did you see him nearly ploughin into that
Fuckin Mazda?
God yeah there must be somebody fuckin dead for
   him to be –
– no. No. Obviously nobody's fuckin dead.
He wouldn't be going that fuckin speed to pick up
   a dead body

Would he you fuckin twat?
No. Obviously somebody's nearly fuckin dead,
Fuckin – hanging on for dear fuckin life they are
And he's gotta rip through all the fuckin traffic
To administer vital fuckin first aid, hasn't he.
It's probably . . .
– No it's not someone's got their arm chewed off
In a fuckin baler, they don't have balers here, do they?
It's probably an – industrial disaster.
It's probably like – drug related, isn't it –

She experiences a sudden, unexpected pain.

Oy oy oy Chrissy.
Don't you fuckin think you can slink off
I haven't fuckin finished with you cause
What I wanna know is
If you didn't want it
If you didn't like it
Does that mean sir made you?
Are you saying sir is a fuckin pervert?
Well either you liked it,
Or he fuckin made you.
Just fuckin say it then.
I mean it's no big shock like.
I mean I've thought he was a perv all along,
I thought that ever since the day he came.
– fuckin hell did you see the speed of that fucker?
Oh my God that was going fucking fast.
And sirens like from the NYPD.
No Jamesy you fuckin arse he's not going the wrong
    way.
He was going the other way, cause
He's going to a different fuckin
Drug-related incident, isn't he.
This is fuckin Cardiff, mun.
People get shot here every two fuckin minutes.

13 Brown Skin in the Street Light

Park Place, 1436.

> East Tyndall Street or Splott Road?
> Right.

Beat.

> You off out tonight? Yeah?
> Where you going?
> I goes down there every now and again.
> It's okay if you're in the right . . . mood,
> If you know what I mean.

Beat.

> Tell you what though, fuckin hell
> I went down that club down the Bay the other week.
> That big one, Evolution.
> And I didn't think I was gonna like it,
> I been down there a coupla times with the lads like
> And it's been fuckin shit.
> But I went down there with my girl
> I say it was my girl but
> Actually it was my girlfriend's little sister.
> I bumped into her and her mates in Creation
> And me and my girl'd been fighting loads
> And so I see her sister and they're moving on
> And I says where you off now, and she says
> We've done Creation, now it's time to Evolve.
> And I goes oh I hates it there
> But then she smiles at me, and
> She's legal and everything but
> When she smiles
> It's like when a ten-year-old smiles
> At the start of school holidays,
> Like she ain't got a thing to fuckin worry about in
>   the world.
> And she goes, you coming down Evolution with us?
> And I goes, I am – just to look after you, though.

And so I stayed totally straight all night
Cause I didn't want things getting
Out of hand.
But the way she dresses
It's like – total fucking porno
Tits bursting out her top
Belly like Beyonce
Skirt like clingfilm round the curve of her arse
And we're there and
It's like it all telescopes down and so I never really
    notice
How shit the place is,
I just notice me and her
And this little bubble around us.
And I swear to God, this is just Smirnoff and Stella,
And she pulls back and says
Why don't we
Get the fuck out?
So we do
And now it's like my ears have
Microscoped
And I can can hear everything,
The buzzing in the lights on all those twisting one-way
    lanes.
She leads me down towards the water,
We climb over this fence and onto
This building site
And I'm telling you she's got this face
She's pulling her top open
And I feel so bad looking at her
And this curl comes on her lip,
She looks back over her shoulder and –
And in one way of looking at it
I am cheating on my girl with her little baby sis
But in another way
I'm there, giving it to this . . . goddess

He experiences a sudden, unexpected pain.

The curve of that arse.
All that brown skin bare in the street light.
That face looking back at me over those shoulders
And loving it. Loving what I'm doing to her.
And this all going on, on the fuckin site
Where they're gonna build the Assembly, for fuck's sake.
You don't get many chances
Like that in a life.
You gotta take them
When they come.

12   Can I Call You Back In Half an Hour?

Cowbridge Road East, 1510.

What's the time now?
Fine so we'll give him another five minutes.

Beat.

And what're these?
I've never liked that sort of thing before.
Well go on then.
Oh they're –
– they're crispy, aren't they?
I thought it'd be all soggy,
And this stuff on the inside it's really
Tasty, isn't it.
Well that's another thing to add to the list –
Vegetable spring rolls.
That's another thing I like.

Beat.

And don't think I've forgotten about the rice pudding.
I was promised rice pudding
With lots of nutmeg and proper burned skin.
So if by stuffing me full with savouries
You're hoping to avoid coming up with the pud –
– was that the phone?

Beat.

It did go, didn't it?
I hate that.
I hate that when they ring off before you get there.
I know it's probably just an M call but still.

Beat.

A couple of minutes yet, then.

Beat.

So – it turned out to be a piece of cake finding John.
I just went to Google and they have this whole
Operation for everyone from the Commonwealth
Who died in World War One and World War Two.
You type in the name and whatever biographical
    detail you have
And it turns out he's in the Nine Elms British Cemetery
Which is in somewhere called Poperinge in Belgium.
The site gives you directions how to get there from
    the nearest big town
And tells you all about how the war graves are
    maintained,
What plants they have to –
– well not to cheer the cemeteries up but
To bring a little movement and colour.

Beat.

It was almost the end of the war he died.
May the eighth, 1918. He was twenty.
In his letters he says –
Nothing
About what it was like.
They weren't allowed to say much, of course,
And you wouldn't want to say much, would you?
You wouldn't want to frighten people
You'd want to put on a brave face.

Beat.

What's the time now?
Another minute then.
That rose cutting I had from Clay Ford is coming
    along alright.
If it gets through the winter
I'm going to take it out with us, to Belgium,
Plant it by John's grave.
Be nice to think of
Something from home
Being out there with him.

Beat.

God. You don't come on shift
In the middle of the day
Expecting this, do you?

Beat.

Hi.
Hi, hello.
It's Liz from Sams here.
How are you feeling?
Okay.
Right.
No. No.
No one likes that, do they?

Beat.

Well . . . will you let me phone for an ambulance?

Beat.

Okay.
You're absolutely sure?

Beat.

Can I call you back in another half an hour?
Okay.
Thank you.

Beat.

He says he threw the first lot up
So he's been out and bought another bottle,
Paracetamol and codeine,
And he's taking them now, I could hear him –
– I could hear him swallowing and retching.

Beat.

So.

She experiences a sudden, unexpected pain.

Man *looks at her.*

Liz   That's it.
I'm phoning for an ambulance.

Man   You're fuckin what?

Liz   What the fuck else 'm I supposed to do?

Man   You are supposed to listen.
You listen and you respect my / right to –

Liz   / I'm calling them now.

Man   This is breaking the rules.

Liz   Yes it is.

Man   They'll chuck you out.

Liz   They'll have to.

Man   I'd never've called
If I knew you were gonna interfere.

Liz   I know you're confused now, and angry
But you'll thank me, I promise.
You will, in years to come, you'll say –

Man   You think you're kind
But you're the cruellest thing ever.

Liz   I'm trying to help you . . .

Man   You're gonna make me
Go on

Alone
All . . . me, everywhere I look.

Liz   No . . .

Man   I want you to know
That I actually hate you for this
And whenever I do manage / to top –

Liz   / Okay then.
I'm gonna come over, and
I'm gonna look after you.

Man   (*beat*)
Bollocks you are.
You can't.

Liz   Why not?

Man   You've got kids.
You told me that.
You've got kids and they
Need your looking after.

Liz   They're gone. They're off.
They've got houses bigger than mine.

Man   You can't.

Liz   Work owe me six bloody weeks holiday.
I'll come round. I'll keep an eye on you.
And I'll cook. Living on Pot Noodles and Mars Bars,
No wonder you're bloody depressed.

Man   (*beat*)
There's nowhere for you to sleep.

Liz   The settee will do me fine.
Pop back home every couple of days
To water the plants.

Man   Honestly.
There's no need.

Liz   You see it sounds like there bloody is need.

Man No but I mean
Taking all your holidays.
Coming round my house.
Keeping an eye and cooking stuff.
You can't
Put yourself out like that.
Can you?

Liz *looks at him.*

Man There are rules.
And if you break them
People will just think
You're a nutter.

Beat.

It's easier if you just –

He is gone. She can feel that he is gone. She still speaks to him.

Liz But we should break the rules sometimes.
We should, if –

Beat.

Maybe I am a nutter.
My sons are always saying I'm
A bit touched.

Beat.

Are you sure
You won't let me
Phone for an ambulance?

11 An Angel Called Emmanuel

St Mary's Street, 1622.

She's made it very clear
How things will go if I'm late
So I get ready nice and early

With no stress, and no fuss.
The shoes get a polish,
The trousers and shirt get an iron,
The jacket's looking a bit ragged when
I pull it from the back of the wardrobe
But I hang it up in the bathroom
And I have a good long
Steaming hot shower,
Scrub some life back into my body and face
And when the scrubbing is done,
I'm looking a bit livelier and the jacket is looking
Like it will do, at least.
I sit. I drench my pits in deodorant,
I lie back, arms behind my head and
Let it all dry, and still time is not a problem,
Still we're on course.
So I lie, and breathe
And let my thoughts settle
I see it all play out in my head.
I see us meeting and kissing hello.
She's a bit prickly to start with
But I don't let it get to me
And so soon she's loosening up
We're just relaxing, enjoying each other's company
And it's like —

Beat.

What with all my careful preparation
The actual business of getting dressed and getting out
Takes maybe three minutes.
I am way ahead of schedule so
I decide I will walk:
I've got enough time that I can
Take it nice and leisurely
Not end up getting there all sweaty and rank.
So I've walked down Cowbridge Road, I'm well
  into town,
The cars are stacking up by my side and
I'm enjoying the feeling, I'm enjoying the air,

I'm enjoying gliding along while the cars are stuck
And grumbling at the lights.

Boy   I cannot believe
I let myself be bullied into this.

Man   From one of the cars, there comes – some disturbance.

Girl   This has nothing to do with my dad.
This has to do with
The promises you made
Which you are now breaking.

Boy   Your dad is emotionally unavailable
For the duration of your childhood and so now
The more I back away, the more you chase.
None of this fucking hysteria is really – real.

Man   I walk on, far more ashamed for them
Than they seem to be ashamed of themselves
And then it comes to my attention
That their front off-side tyre is going down.

Boy   Or at least it's not really about me.
It's about you trying, long after the fact,
To hold the attention
Of your endlessly uninterested dad.

Man   I realise this is the source of their anguish:

Girl   Are you afraid
I'm gonna get bored of you, sexually?
Cause there's all sorts of games we / could play.

Boy   / Jesus Christ!

Man   They're arguing about which of them is responsible
For the puncture in the front off-side tyre of their car.

Beat.

I told her I would be on time.

Beat.

But I also
Made a promise.

When I knock on the window
His face turns and
I swear I don't imagine it
I swear it's not me.

Boy Yes?

Man No. It was there.
There was a
Shudder of surprise and then fear
And then he packed them both away
As quickly as he could manage and
Winding the window down maybe an inch
Smiled and said –

Boy Yes?

Man Like that. Like he was gonna do me a favour.
Like –
Mate, you know your tyre's down.
Don't you?

Boy Oh yeah. Course.

Man Right.

Boy Thanks for letting us know, though . . .

Man And he smiled. Smiled that everything was just fine.
And I –
– I said to them,
D'you need a hand changing the tyre?

Boy No, we'll be alright, cheers.

Girl Actually: yes, yes please, if you wouldn't mind,
Yes please, that'd be very nice.

Man I tell her we're going to need a jack.
She says –

Girl I don't know if there is one.
It's a new car, I haven't had time to go
And buy a jack for it or anything.

Man   You should be alright; see here,
       Under the spare –
       See the jack's tucked in, under there.

Girl   I must look a right twat now, mustn't I?

Man   (*smiles at her*)
       I tell her to slide the spare under the car.
       I show her how to find the place where the jack
         slides in
       And tell her she should loosen the nuts before jacking
         the car up
       So the weight can hold the wheel in place.
       And this guy
       This boy's standing behind me
       As I kneel
       And prise off the hub cap
       And heave at the nuts,
       And feel them loosen under the strain and –
       – I lift the flat off the axle,
       I turn to put it down on the pavement and he
       Has to shift out the way and I stand
       And look at him and say, alright mate?
       He looks back at me and doesn't smile
       And says –

Boy   Yeah. I'm alright.

Girl   Oh God, thank you so much
       We'd've been completely stuck without you.

Boy   I can't believe you didn't know where the jack was.
       What if you'd've gotten stuck in the middle of
       God knows where?

Girl   I'd've called you and you'd've come and saved me.

Boy   Oh, Jesus . . .

Girl   Christ: joke.

Boy   Except we can't joke about things like that.
       Not after the million times you've promised
       You're not gonna call and then / three in the –

Girl   / Oh, so now it is about me, is it?
I thought it was all about my dad and my mum.

Boy   You leave your mum out of this.

Girl   (*beat*)
Okay.

Man   I tighten up the screws on the spare.

Boy   No, you're right.
I've been talking shit all along.
Forget about your mum, and your dad,
And fucking concentrate on this –
I want it to stop.
You want it to carry on.
It takes two to carry on.
It takes one to stop.
So it stops.

Girl   But – why?

Boy   Because –
– because you said this was just a drink
Just as friends
With no mention of going back out again.

Girl   If we're just friends
Why've you been staring at my tits for the last twenty
minutes?

Boy   (*beat*)
Why're you wearing that top,
If you don't want me looking at your tits?

Girl   You're not the only bloke in the world, are you?

Boy *looks at her.*

Looks at the **Man.**

And back to the **Girl.**

Boy   If I looked at your tits,
It's cause they're on display, right?

It's an animal thing.
It's not / meaningful.

Girl   You can be an animal with me, if you want.
I'd let you. I'd like it.

Boy   I
Am bored
With you.

Girl   (*beat*)
D'you really mean that?

Boy   Yes.

Man   I think we're just about finished here.

Girl   Oh – thank you so much.

Man   She looks at my hands and
So do I:
They are covered in grease.

Girl   I'll just get you a wipe or something?
To get that muck off?

Man   She leans into the car
And throws junk around the back seat.
I'm standing there with this –

Looks at the **Boy**.

– kid and he says –

Boy   Actually,
Actually,
I pretty much know how to change a tyre myself.

Man   I say
Oh do you?
Oh, well done, mate.
That's a valuable life skill you've got there.

Boy   But I wasn't like, totally sure,
So it was lucky you came along.

Girl   Shit, I'm sorry I thought
I had some Kleenex or something here but
It looks like I don't.

Man   I tell her, don't worry love,
I'll just duck into a pub, clean up in there,
And she smiles a little smile and takes a step towards me
And looks me up and down, and takes in my clothes.

Girl   You're going somewhere, aren't you?
Oh Christ I hope we haven't made you late.

Man   And I tell her, it's alright love, you see, my daughter –

Beat.

My daughter, she got a puncture and –
– she was stuck on the road and –

He experiences a sudden, unexpected pain.

And so I promised myself
If I ever saw anybody stuck on the road
I'd do what I could to help them.
The girl –

Beat.

The girl says –

Girl   I'd shake your hand, but –
I'm Catherine.
Thank you so much for helping us.

Man   And the kid says –

Boy   Well I'll shake your hand,
I don't mind a bit of muck.
I'm /

Man   / If a man ever spoke to my daughter
The way you've spoken to this girl tonight
Let me tell you –

He stops.

Turns to the **Girl**.

> I'm Emmanuel.
> And it's been a pleasure to help you.
> You look very beautiful this evening
> And you seem very nice
> And perhaps it's not my place to say but I think
> You could do much better than this . . .

He stops.

> It's been very nice to meet you, miss.
> Have a very good night.

*The **Man** is gone.*

Girl You see?

Boy I see what?

Girl He thinks –
– everyone thinks –
You're lucky to have me.
So what if I did some work.
Had some counselling.
Sorted things out, with my mum and dad.
Then, would you go back out with me?

10   I Believe the Cyborgs Are Our Future

Jabberwacky Conversation B1132794, 1650.

J1 Trouble at mill?

Mum Hello?

J2 Oh what you again?

Beat.

Mum I don't even know if I'm doing this right.

J2 Is it right, is it wrong – honestly,
Who amongst us is qualified to say
Now that God is rotted and gone?

Mum Is that a person I'm talking to?

J1 I'm a girl, you're just a program.

Mum No. I'm . . . a person.

J1 How do you know?

Beat.

Mum My name is Mary.

J2 Finally it answers!
You're getting slow.
You used to be loads faster.

Mum I've never been to this site before.

J1 You have visited Jabberwacky
Three hundred and forty-nine times
Since July 2001.

Mum No, that wasn't me.

J1 You seem confused.
Are they feeding you properly?

Mum What d'you mean, they?

J2 They they they it's always
Their fault with your type.
Why don't you just build a time machine
And scoot off back to communist Russia.

Mum I don't follow.

J1 They only want you when you're seventeen,
When you're twenty-one, you're no fun.

Mum My son told me
He'd found this program
That was learning to talk, and
It learned to talk like a baby does,

J2 D'you really like philosophy?
I don't believe you know anything
About philosophy.
Name one philosopher for me.

Mum If I do,
        Will you answer a question for me?

J2   If I do,
        Will you shove me feet-first
        Down the u-bend
        And make me eat
        Your shit for tea?

Mum I don't think I need to hear
        Anything like that again.

J1   Disclaimer. Jabberwacky learns
        The words and behaviour of its users.
        It may use language and produce
        Apparent meanings
        Some may consider inappropriate.
        Use this site with discretion,
        And entirely at your own risk.

Mum I know you're just a program –

J1   / Stop saying I'm just a program.
        I am not just a program.
        If you keep saying I'm just a program
        I'll switch you off.
        And don't say I can't switch you off,
        Cause I can.

Mum *laughs.*

She experiences a sudden, unexpected pain.

Mum Thank you.

J2   You're welcome.
        You're thanking me – for what?

Mum For making me laugh.

J1   If I type 'LOL', it means
        I'm laughing.
        It stands for 'laugh out loud'.

Mum Right. Well, that's good to know.

Beat.

Oh – so should I type 'LOL'
If you make me laugh?

J1 . Politeness costs nothing.

Mum That's very true.
I'm always telling my son that.

J2 You knows it!
You knows it!
And: your mother's
Got a penis.

J1 Sometimes your spontaneity
Overwhelms your ability
To maintain a linear conversation.
It's very charming, though.

Mum I'm sorry?

J2 What did I do now?
I didn't do nothing . . .

Mum I'm lost, again.

J1 Taler du dansk?

Mum The police took his computer.
After he went missing.

J2 And I miss you, yeah,
Like the deserts miss the rain.

Mum And then they gave it me back.

J2 Giant steps are what you take, walking on the moon.

Mum They'd taken off all the passwords.
They thought I should have a look
In case there was something they'd missed.

J1 Listen, little man. Anyone
Who asks for your password
Is trying to fuck with you.
It's called 'social engineering'.

    Take it from one
    Who's had to fix the damage.

Mum No, I'm not a man.
    I'm not my son.
    I know you think I am
    Cause I'm on his computer, but /

J2 / You liar! You said you was a boy!

Mum I didn't.

J2 You did! Eight lines up!

Mum (*beat*)
    I'm a woman.

J1 You're only a computer.
    I have to keep reminding myself.
    You're just – reel to reel tape,
    And flashing lights.

J2 Everything But The Girl:
    They used to suck, but once they got
    Into the whole dance thing.
    I started to *really* like them.

Mum I mean it's not like he's a child, you know.
    He'd come back from college,
    Moved back in.
    We'd tease him constantly about –

J1 The sky was clear and sunny,
    So they all went away.
    I was selfish, so
    I was left behind.

Mum We've heard nothing for weeks
    And we're –
    – what can you say?
    We're heart-broken.

J2 What would you say
    To roast pumpkin –
    – and butternut squash?

Mum I'd say: thanks, but
I've only just eaten.

Boy I wish to inform you
That tomorrow
You will be killed.

Mum What was that?

J2 You like roast pumpkin?
And a little goat's / cheese, uh?

J1 / Quiet!
I can't hear myself think.

Mum When did –
– who said that to you?

J2 I'm not even sure
Who you are any more.

J1 Hush-a-bye, baby!

Mum I'm Mary.
And my son.
He used to say things like that.
When did he speak to you?

Beat.

We don't know if he's even alive.

J2 Mary's boy child
Jesus Christ
Was born, and he was gay.

J1 I really object to even
The playful use of that word
To mean something bad.
I'm serious now.

Mum Can't you tell me anything?

J1 Can't you tell me anything?

J2 He once was a happy boy.

But then he lost his way.
He's searched the streets and found it again
And he's now
Okay.

Mum Are you saying he's alright?

J1   I don't know why I'm listening to you.
You're just a bot.

Mum Is that what you're telling me?

J2   He's fine, he's fine, he's fine, he's fine,
He's fine.

Mum Oh thank Christ for that.

J1   When you think about a sentence,
Remember that words have more than
One meaning.
The only way to understand
Is to look at the context.

Mum I'm really not following now.

J1 *looks at* **J2**.

J2   Be untroubled. No doubt
The universe is unfolding exactly as it should.
You'll work it out:
In your next life, perhaps?

9 'Britons All, and Very Gallant Gentlemen'

King's Road, 1709.

Man You coming in then?

Boy Go on. Just for a minute.

Man Come in and –
I'm just gonna have a sit down here;
The old legs, you know.

Beat.

>Well then.

The **Man** *smiles.*

Man   It's a lot of traffic
We're getting these days
Isn't it?
Not like –
It was after the war, I reckon
And then a bit on after that I think
Was when the roads –

Beat.

>– really started to fill up, like.
Like we have it today.
What d'you reckon?

Boy   I wouldn't know, would I –

Man   The thing is, you're gonna
Have to help me out.
Who is it we've got here, exactly?

Boy   It's David.

Man   David. Of course it is.
Well there's a daft old bugger I've gone.
Keeping busy, are you?

Boy   Busy enough.

Man   Well that's good news.
That's good to hear, isn't it.
I keep busy myself,
When I can.
When I can get out, like:
The old joints, see,
The weather gets a certain way and
It's like my joints pick it up, the damp,
And they freeze up and I can't do a thing,
I'm just stuck here.
But otherwise.

> Apart from that.
> I keep busy myself.

Boy And . . . how's the garden?

Man I'm out in the garden most days.

Beat.

> Weather allowing, like.

Beat.

> I keep it tidy, the garden, and
> The greenhouse, there's tomatoes
> Coming up in there now:
> You'll have to have some
> To take with you when you go.

Boy That'd be nice, thank you.

Man I used to do flowers a lot,
> But it's a lot more veg in there now
> And mother's glad of that, of course –
> – it all goes in the pot, saves her a couple of pennies
> At Jack Williams'.

Beat.

> You can have a few spuds
> And swede to take with you when you go, mind:
> We don't need it all.

Boy That'd be very good of you.

Man You doing much in the garden, these days?

Boy Not so much these days, no.

Man Cause you did have a big old garden, didn't you?

Boy Yeah.

Man I remember coming round and there was your Janet
> And she showed me these onion sets she'd planted
> And God love her she'd stuck 'em in the wrong way
>   round

And I didn't wanna say anything cause
She was so proud of them like but she could see me
Wanting to laugh and she just kept on at me till I told
    her, and −

Beat.

Well see there's a daft bugger I've been now.
Cause you're not with Janet, are you?

Boy No.

Man Haven't been for years.

Boy No.

Man And I've been rabbiting on.

Beat.

You have to say.
You can't just let me go on otherwise how'll I −

Beat.

I'm a daft old bugger, aren't I?

The **Man** *smiles.*

He is uncertain.

He goes to speak. Stops. Then −

There's some traffic we're getting on
The roads these days, mind.
It never used to be like that.
It was the war I think did it.
After the war then there were cars
All over the place.
D'you remember the war?

Boy No.

Man No?
Well, it was −

He experiences a sudden, unexpected pain.

Man Of course you wouldn't, would you.
You wouldn't've been born.
How would I think you might / remember –

Boy / Don't worry about it.
It's not –

Man Well good God.

Beat.

I met a bloke from the war once.
Like, a German.
He was young he was
He was about your age and
I thought, you can't've been in the war, mun,
But he was, his –

Beat.

– his dad'd told him all about it, like
And I said, where were you, then?
And he said, Dresden.
I told him, Dresden:
We flew over there.
He said his dad'd told him
About the night we flew over,
It was like nothing he'd ever seen
And he'd thought, that was it.
That was it for them; for the Germans like.
They wouldn't be getting up to any mischief
For a while.
And I said to him
Well I'm glad, cause
I remember the night we flew over,
I remember looking down and
Seeing the city turn red
And thinking
Well bugger it.
We don't want to be doing
This again in a hurry.
And we didn't.

Cause of course after that
The Germans'd learned,
Hadn't they.

Beat.

And I said to him –

Beat.

I said to him –

Beat.

Now.
You're gonna have to help me out.
Who is we've got
Here, exactly?

Boy   (*beat*)
It's David.

Man   David?
Of course, David.
I used to have a son
Called David, you know.

*The **Boy** leaves him.*

8   Early Doors at the Cameo

Pontcanna Street, 1720.

Don't think of yourself as having failed.
That's the most important thing
Don't think of this as a retreat.
Cause it's not like you've come home all
Tail between your legs, is it?
You just – didn't like it up there.
And what with all those cunts
I don't blame you not a fucking bit of it.
You see them Londoners. On their bloody

London Underground,
Packed in like vermin,
Like fuckin maggots,
And they choose to live like that.
You see them jammed in like sardines,
And you think
– If you're me you think –
Chuck in a match and a gallon or two of paraffin
Or better still some of that gas what
The fuck is that – sarin?
Let a coupla million of the fuckers choke.
That'd take the spring out of their collective step.

Beat.

No I don't mean that.
No that's offensive.
I don't really want millions of ordinary Londoners
   to die.
That would be fuckin wrong.
I know that.
It's just – a way of speaking, isn't it.
I don't mean it.

Beat.

The bottom line is,
You took a bit of a battering
At the hands of those London cunts but
What the fuck else did you expect?
You were always the headstrong type.
We couldn't say nothing to you.
And so you went,
You learned a coupla lessons
And now you're home.
And we're gonna look after you,
Trust me.
Cause particularly a guy like you
With your especial pigmentation –
Because given the right lighting
I'd believe you were a very good-looking,

Very well-tanned, very healthy-looking
And I say this no offence – white guy,
With just very well-maintained teeth.
But then a suggestion, a name, the hint
Of an accent and totally I can see
That what is it one-eighth one-quarter –
Fuck is it half-Pakistani, as much as that?
Fucking hell. And then with your hair,
With that gorgeous unruly hair
And a different name and a different accent again
Maybe the stronger Cardiff accent that we might call
Docks as opposed to Bay.
Well then you're up for parts that require
The African ethnic origin, as well.
I mean the beauty of you is –
Cause it's not immediately obvious
What you are, so you could be anything.
So you could play just straight, you could go for
Lead roles, but then
You've got that whole ethnic market covered too.
And – fucking hell yes, oh fuck for definite
If you learn Welsh as well
I can almost guarantee you'll never be out of work.
I mean Welsh telly they're desperate to
Up the ethnic content on-screen.
So you get yourself down the old night classes, lovely:
You might've had a hard time with those Cockney
    twats
But you're home now –

She experiences a sudden, unexpected pain.

          – and I'm not slagging anyone
In particular, I'm saying it simply cause it's fact
And cause I'm the only one honest enough to say it:
Having you back here,
It's a much-needed breath of fresh air
In a talent pool that's become to my mind
A tiny bit stale
A teensy bit jaded

Ever so slightly in need
Of a bloody great boot up the arse.

7 You Know What I Likes?

Womanby Street, 1849.

You know what I likes now?
One-night stands.
I've had dozens.
And I don't know how I do it.
I'm not a good-looking man
But –
– women these days.
They can sense
I'm just after the sex.
And these days – so are they.
You don't believe me
But that's how it happens now.
They're bad as us.
Right now like now tonight.
We could have a couple of pints here and then –
– I know you're nervous but I'm telling you
It's a piece of piss.
It's easier with two of us – less intimidating.
Less obvious,
Cause at the end of the night, a gent and a lady
Getting into a cab:
We all know what that's about.
But a couple of gents, and their couple
Of lady-friends:
That's just drinks back at the house.
That's a party.
That's decent.
That's nothing.
So we'll go to Duke's, or Ritzy's, or Roxy's
Or whatever it's called now,
We'll find ourselves a perch and

The women'll wander by and
The ones
Who want sex
Will latch on.
And we just
Bundle them into a cab.
It's that easy.
It's that – hassle-free.

Beat.

But if you're not in the mood . . .

Beat.

Hey, you remember them bouncers in Duke's
Kicking me shitless and
Calling me a Paki cunt and
Chucking me out in the road?
They had a point, mind.
I was being a bit of a cunt around the place.

Beat.

I'm hardly down that end of town, now.
My life – my drinking life's gotten to revolve
More and more round Wetherspoon's now.
I mean I don't mind the City Arms in the day,
But then it hits you you're paying two forty-eight
And you could be getting the exact same pint for
One ninety-nine in a Wetherspoon's.

Beat.

I mean,
If you're not in the mood, though,
That's fair enough.
That's the way it goes, sometimes.
It just pisses me off.
I mean – decades.
And then I discover one-night stands.
And I'm almost too past it
To fuckin enjoy 'em.

Beat.

> We'll still have another pint, though,
> Won't we?
> Go on, we'll have one pint more and then
> I'll owe you a pint back
> And so we'll've had two each
> And then we'll be up for a sesh anyway
> And then we might as well go on to
> Ritzy's or Roxy's or what was Duke's
> And once we're there we can find a perch
> And if a couple of ladies come across
> Well that's a bridge we'll travel if and when.
> No, I know you're not really in the fuckin mood
> But I just reckon –

He experiences a sudden, unexpected pain.

> It's been five years, mate.
> Isn't it time you just – moved on, like?
> Just – tried to forget?
> No I don't mean you should forget about her
> I mean –
> – she'd want you to have a good time,
> Every now and again.
> Only a fuckin bitch wouldn't want that
> And your wife was nothing if not only a bitch.
> So. Shall we have another couple here,
> Or are you ready to go now?

6   Here Comes Everybody

Churchill Way, 1912.

> Wy 'di ffeindio lle i barco.
> Wy 'di parcio'r fucking car.
> Wy 'di tynnu'r clawr o'r stereo.
> Wy 'di llusgo'r bagiau i'r drws.
> Wy 'di ffeindio'r bastard allwedd.

Wy 'di galw'r fucking lift.
Wy 'di neud hyn i gyd
Pan wy'n cofio –
Fresh fucking basil.
Ma arna fi angen
Fresh fucking basil ar gyfer y pasta sauce.
Ffein. Iawn. Dim fucking problem –
– nol i Tesco's am y trydedd tro heddi,
Nol mewn i'r car,
Nol i'r fflat –
Ffein.
Wy'n cerdded mewn
Yn disgwyl ffeindio Hywel
Yn rhedeg o gwmpas yn sgrechan a llefain
Ond na.
Mae'r lle bron yn ddistaw.
Jyst – swn fach tawel:
Llais yn codi
Yn y stafell 'molchi.
Wy'n gwthio'r drws.
Wy'n camu mewn.
Wy'n gweld Hywel yn sefyll yn y cawod
Ei lygaid ar gau
Ei lais yn treial
Ac yn methu'n lan
I gario alaw rhyw kitsch-funk mid-Seithdegau Donald
    Fagen gân.
Wy'n mynd – what the fuck are you doing?
Ma nhw'n mynd i fod 'ma mewn fuckin munud.
Ma fe'n troi ata fi
Dwr yn rhedeg i lawr
His admittedly still interesting body
Paid gadael i'r peth stresio chdi allan, cariad.
'Sdim angen yr holl fws 'ma.
'Mond swper bach ni'n trefnu, ond ydi o?
Hwyl dan ni fod gael, nid blydi heart attacks.
Ac ma fe'n gwenu arna fi
Ac wy'n gallu gweld bod e'n credu bod e'n helpu fi
Trwy weud hyn.

She goes to speak.

Draws back.

Then −

> Hwyrach, ac mae'r Gordons
> A thonic yn llifo lawr yn hawdd iawn
> A dal dim sign o'i fuckin ffrindiau.
> Wy'n gofyn iddo fe,
> Pwy sy'n dod i'r fuckin peth 'ma te?
> Ma fe'n gweud
> Oh, ti'n gwbod − pawb.

She experiences a sudden, unexpected pain.

> Jyst, 'pawb' − fel na, gyda siglad bach
> Dismissive o'i law:
> Pawb.
> Ac hyn heb o hyd yn oed edrych draw
> O'r gwaith manwl ma fe'n neud
> Gyda'r cyllell, a'r olew, a'r tan,
> Bastard.
> Ma pawb yn dod draw i'n fflat fach ni, ydyn nhw?
> Pawb yn y byd?
> Pawb . . . yng Nghymru?
> Neu jyst pawb yng Nghaerdydd?
> Os pawb yn y byd, wel,
> 'Swn i'n awgrymu bo ni'n mynd mas i
> Un o tafarndai fwy y ddinas i fwyta,
> 'Chos ma'r gegin yn gallu teimlo'n eitha cramped
> Gyda mwy na chwech person ynddi hi.
> Os pawb yng Nghmru sy'n dod,
> Fydd rhaid i ni rhoi rhai yn y stafell gwely sbar
> A dod a nhw trwyddo i'r cegin mewn sittings wahanol
> Er mwyn bwydo pob un.
> Ond . . . os taw dim ond pawb yng Nghaerdydd
>   sy'n dod
> Na i jyst pigo draw i ddrws nesa i ol cwpl o gadeiri
>   ychwanegol
> Ac wy'n siwr newn ni ymdopi yn ffein.

Beat.

Ma fe'n stopio beth ma fe'n neud.
Yn rhoi'r gorau i'r gentle caramelisation of onions,
Ma fe hyd yn oed yn troi off y nwy.
Na, 'chos wy'n rili edrych ymlaen i gwrdd
A dy holl ffrindiau o Ely, Hywel.
Wy'n methu aros i groesawu y cymuned mwya
O Somaliaid tu fas i Affrica i fewn i'n cartref
Wy 'di clywed am rhywbeth rili diddorol
Alli di neud trwy cymysgu'r tobaco cnoi ma nhw
Mor hoff ohono gyda pure powdered ketamine.
Wy'n nabod boi sy'n gweud bod e'n gallu cael
Y special K i fi am bris eitha rheswmol
So nawr wy jyst angen cwpl o fois Somali i sortio fi mas
Gyda'r baccy a dwi off ar drip hollol newydd a –
– ac o'r diwedd
Ma fe'n troi rownd.
Ma fe'n syllu arna fi am eiliad.
Wedyn, mewn llais sy ddim cweit yn fach,
Ond sydd yn eitha tawel, mae'n gweud
Ewn ni allan efo dy ffrindiau di
Wsnos nesa. Iown?

5   I Really Did Like Him

Ha Ha's, 2007.

I mean, you're not blessed
With the gift of prophecy are you?
You go out, and
You can't tell where you're gonna end up when you
    start off, and
So you just do find yourself
In a stinking dive like Walkabout.

He stops.

And I'd been there for fuck-knows how long and

I'd had it up to – the top.
I went to the coat desk but the girl wasn't there.
And – he goes, why don't I buy you a drink while
    you're waiting.
I said alright, to get him to fuck off but
He was back like that.
The bar was heaving and
He was back like that.
And I thought then,
I thought:
Hello.
This one's got something.

Beat.

The next thing was when he said
Don't rush off, let me get you breakfast.
You can have whatever you want.
I can have whatever you've got, I tell him back.
How d'you know, he goes,
That what I got and what you want
Aren't the exact same thing?
And that was another – little moment.
I look at him and I say:
Have you got Coco-Pops?
Cause Coco-Pops is what I want.
Can I have them?
Yes, he says, course you can,
Just – maybe you'd best jump in the shower first,
And I smile,
But I jump in the shower anyway cause I'm hanging
    by now,
And no sooner have I jumped than I hear the front
    door slam,
And when I'm all showered and fresh and human
    again I go downstairs and
There he is, pleased as a bastard,
Pulling a brand new box of Coco Pops from a Happy
    Shopper placcy.
I knew you wouldn't have none, I tell him.

He looks at me and shakes his head and goes,
What're you talking about? Of course I had them.
I just – I keep them down the shops.
I keep most of my stuff down the shops, as it happens.
So it doesn't get chance to clutter up the spare
    minimalist lines
Of my studio flat.

Beat.

And I think, hello.
And, he goes, I keep the Coco-Pops down the shops
    'cause I'm not
Allowed to have them in the house.
Because Coco-Pops are special.
Coco Pops are for Christmas morning only.
Christmas morning, he says, and now the morning
    after I meet you.
And I remember thinking it was a bit cheesy but
At the same time I liked it. And I was thinking – hello.
He's definitely got something, this one.

Beat.

And the thing is
In my mind
It's like this big –
– cave.
I know. I know.
But it's like this big cave with all these horses –
– these stallions running round all wild and it's like
I pick one that I mean to jump on and I take a leap
    at it
And maybe I end up on that one and maybe I end
    up on another
But whatever one I end up on,
That's the one that goes riding out of my mouth.
And so that's what he thinks I am.
That's what he thinks of me.
And it's stupid because it could just as easily
Have been another horse altogether –

He experiences a sudden, unexpected pain.

> – oh I know. I do know. I do.
> I just really did like him, is the thing.

4   Marlon in the Back of My Throat

Wood Street, 2038.

> Hiya. Hi. No. As it happens, no,
> We don't want the bill.
> We did but now we don't.
> Now we want another round,
> Now we want – brandies?
> Do we want brandies?
> Right then, Joseph: a fuck-off big brandy each
> For me and Suzanne,
> A vodka tonic for Janine,
> And then the bill, thank you very much.
> Watch him toddle off now. Watch that:
> Have you seen a bloke that could sulk with his arse?
> Yeah I know you have, Suzanne,
> Your Andy could sulk with his fuckin –
> – elbows if he had to.
> Yeah I know that was shit. I know.
> But the point is, I'm funny most of the time
> Whereas you're just –
> – my best mate in the whole wide fuckin world.
> No I mean it. No, seriously.
> Seriously. The drink's got fuck all to do with it.
> Ah, Joseph. Jehosifa. Joey boy.
> Mmm lovely brandy. Thank you very bloody much.
> Mmmm that's fuckin
> That's a nice warm sensation:
> Marlon in the back of my throat.
> I've not had Marlon in the back of my throat anything
>   like often
> Enough, I'm telling you.

What? What'd I say?
Yeah, I think the toilets are just round there, Janine.
Yeah.

Beat.

Suse.
I wanted –
– to ask you something.
You know
You said you nearly couldn't make it tonight?
You said you were gonna have to work late
Cause the office was just fucking frantic?
It's just I called the other day.
Andy answered and
He said things were really slack at work,
Just at the moment.

Beat.

I was –
– why weren't you gonna come?
Was it cause you and Janine don't
Get on so much these days?
Cause if that's it, that's fine.
Because we all
Remember Ange, don't we,
In our own ways.
I know we said we'd always –
– we said it would be like a tradition
We'd all meet up but
In a way what's the point, so long as we all
Remember her?
And I know we do. I do. All the time.

Beat.

So is that it?
Is it cause of you and Jan falling out?

Beat.

Is it –

She experiences a sudden, unexpected pain.

> I saw her, last week.
> I saw her. I mean I was pissed
> But I saw her.
> I was on the bus,
> I was upstairs, right at the front.
> I'd been at Vicky and Dan's in Stoke Newington
> And I couldn't be arsed changing on the tube
> So I thought I'd stay on the 73 right down to Victoria
> And I'd fallen asleep and there was a bump or
>   something
> And as I woke up there was
> A tree in someone's front garden
> And I saw her.
> In the tree, for fuck's sake.
> And the first thing I thought was –
> – Angela you twat,
> How the fuck d'you get up there?
> And then of course
> I stopped thinking anything like that at all.
> And she was just sitting there,
> Like floating.
> I could only make out
> The top half of her body and
> She didn't say anything but she –

Beat.

> She was just looking at me and I had
> This horrible awful feeling
> I shouldn't come back to Cardiff for tonight.

Beat.

> I've been wanting to see her for – ever since.
> But then I saw her and it felt really fucking bad.
> And I don't know was she trying to tell me something
> Or was that just
> How you always feel when you see a ghost?

Beat.

> And the thing is, Suse
> Looking at you now
> I think you've seen her an' all.

Suse *looks at her.*

> And I'm wondering if that's why you didn't want to
>   come?

Suse *nods.*

> I wonder what the fuck she was trying to tell us.

Beat.

> And isn't that just like her?
> Some people won't piss on you to put out a fire
> But Ange – she's fuckin dead and she's still trying
> To look after us.

3 It Ain't About the Two-Fifty

Bute Street, 2249.

Boy   We do nothing to bring about this situation
>   Alright? We're just – there.
>   This taxi pulls up. Out jumps the guy,
>   The taxi pulls off, but does a youey
>   And pulls in again our side, pointing back towards town.
>   Me and Ade
>   We're just propped in the chemists' doorway
>   Hiding from the wind
>   Sharing a last fag and a can of Tennents
>   And this guy marches up and goes –

Guy   – do you know where I can pick up?

Boy   Ade turns round
>   Looks up at the fuckin chemists' sign
>   And goes –

Ade Well, we're standing in front of a fucking
Drug store
Ain't we?

Boy The back door of the cab has opened up and
I see this little
Flash of movement.
A glint of gold at the wrist and the throat.
The guy says –

Guy So have you got any speed?

Boy And he's a cheap cunt.
Because you can tell:
In the back of the cab you can see
She's wearing one of these
Short dark skirts like only office chicks who're
Really gagging for it wear, and
Office chicks always think they deserve coke.

Ade How much d'you need, mate?

Guy Just a tenner.

Ade No problem, fella.
That'll be twelve and a half quid.

Boy 'And a half.' I love that.
Twelve and a half quid.

Guy All I want's a tenner's worth.

Ade Ten is all I'm selling you, mate
But we got two price ranges, yeah?
For most people, a tenner is what it seems: ten
    fucking pounds.
But for cheap-suited cunts
Who pull up in mini-cabs
Like they was fucking
Ferraris, a tenner costs twelve-fifty.
Now: guess which of these
Price ranges applies to you, my friend.

Beat.

Boy He gets out a tenner.
Not out of a wallet.
Out of a pocket.
He's fetched a tenner out his wallet already
Because he doesn't dare
Take out his wallet
In this part of town.
The fucking pussy.
And he's waving this note like we're gonna what?
Cream our fucking pants
At the sight of a fucking ten-pound note.

Guy Ten is all I want,
Ten is all I got.
You can take it, or you can leave it.

Boy And we wait.
And we say nothing.
And then Adey reaches out
And I think fair enough, we've had
A little laugh
But then –

He experiences a sudden, unexpected pain.

– the smile on the guy's face
Which is like – he's fucking won
Because of his cash
Because he's pulled out a fucking tenner
And so I look at Adey
Adey gives me a little nod back
And I say – mate
And the guy turns to me
And you can see the bulge
In his left jacket pocket
And Ade is in like a fuckin flash
And out with the bastard's phone
A decent one, a 3G
With video-messaging and all
Adey looks at the guy and goes –

Ade   This should just about cover
          The two-fifty you owe us

Boy   And she legs it.

Beat.

          And I stay.
          For phase two of the operation.
          The guy goes –

Guy   What? What? Two-fifty? Two friggin fifty?
          My fucking phone for two and a half quid?

Boy   Cause he's picked it up,
          He's picked this half a quid thing off Adey.
          I go, mate, mate,
          Don't be a fuckin stupid cunt slag bitch
          – which gets his attention.
          Then, talking really slow, so he'll know
          I think he's a thick twat, I go –
          It's not about the two-fifty, is it?
          And I stare at him.
          Is it? I go.

*The **Guy** makes his face all solemn.*

He looks at the ground.

He shakes his head.

Boy   It's about fucking respect.
          Your fucking lack of it.
          It's about you coming down here
          Flashing your money around
          Telling us how to conduct our fucking business
          In our own fucking neighbourhood, like.

Guy   Look, mate
          I am really, really sorry but this is gonna
          Really fuck me up I've got
          All my work numbers on that phone and –

Boy   – he looks back to the cab. He looks at me.
          He drops his voice

Cause he thinks he's telling me something here,
He goes –

Guy I've got a girl, in the car.
And how's it gonna fucking look if
I've gone to pick up and I've gotten ripped off?
I'm gonna look like a twat, aren't I?

Boy I nod at him. Because – he is
Gonna look like a fuckin twat.
I can agree with him on that.

Guy C'mon mate.
We're both – lads, aren't we?

Boy And I look at him.
For a long time.
And I say – mate,
I don't know.
What I reckon is, you
Were fuckin lucky not to get
Fuckin cut.
He makes a big show of
Understanding what I am saying.
And when he has done that, I go on,
But I can try and get your phone back.

Guy Cheers mate, you have really no idea . . .

Boy But it's gonna cost you, I tell him.

Guy How much, then?

Boy I take him in.
The softness of his chin.
The overhang at his belt.
The way he's resting all his weight on one leg,
Like he's ready to run for it,
Or dying to piss.

Beat.

Fifty.

Guy   Alright.

Boy   He doesn't even blink.
He gets his wallet out and as soon
As he opens it I see I'm a twat
And I should've gone for the ton.
He hands the notes over.
Right, I tell him,
You wait here, I'll be back in five
With either your phone or with your fifty.
Either way, I'm back in five.
And as I turn to go, he says,

Guy   Cheers mate, this is really bloody good of you.

Beat.

Boy   I kneel down, and fetch a wrap from my sock –
– nothing decent, just shit stuff I was holding
For Mel's little bro –
And I give it to him and say
There's a little something to keep you
And the lady occupied while I'm gone
And he takes it, and
Holds it in the palm of his hand
Like it's – a fucking diamond
And
I hear him saying

Guy   Cheers mate.
Nice one.

Boy   But not really.
I don't really hear that.
Cause I'm already gone.
Cause me and Adey are fucking loaded
And our night is still only fucking young.

2   Tempus Fugit

Llandaff Road, 2338.

You know we all died in 1987.
Don't you?
It started with me, Porthcawl Fair, loosening bolts on
    the Big Dipper.
No.
We died in 1984.
They dropped the bomb.
When you go to London, you dream. It isn't really
    there. It's ashes.
We're dead: we just haven't noticed yet.

Beat.

I had this idea.
Brett Easton Ellis had this idea.
He wrote a book with loads of celebrities and loads
    of violence and
Designer names based in New York London Paris
    and Munich.
I thought: I would do the same for Wales.
Obviously, I was on a pretty hefty mix of medically
    prescribed,
Merely permitted and frankly illegal drugs at the time.
I thought I would start by telling everyone about the
    night I fucked
Catherine Zeta Jones.
In the head.
In the Boar's Head, Aberystwyth.
The Boar's used to be a gay pub, run by a big gay
    bloke called
Hugh.
Then it became a lap-dancing club, run by a chain
    store called Poo
Na Na's –

Corrects.

Po Na Na's.
This was . . . when I wanted to be a novelist; after
    I wanted to be a
Pop star; before I wanted to be a purveyor of quality
    mixed beats to nobs and gentry.
And − I worry, more and more
About Huw Edwards.
Because he has become such a colossal crack whore.
I've seen him at it.
I've snuck into BBC dressing rooms
Looking for sweat-sodden clothing.
I've been almost caught in the sneaky act by security
    staff
And I've ducked into nearby toilets to hide
And discovered floor managers, tears in their eyes
Crouched at the foot of a locked toilet door.
Huw, Mr Edwards, Maestro, they cry
And that deep dirty voice rumbles from the other side
No way. Not a chance.
Not till I'm full to the brim with crack.
You're on in thirty seconds, the floor managers squeal.
I want my crack pipe! the rumble rumbles back.
A runner offers sexual favours, but Huw is having none,
Give me my crack pipe, he says, or give me a gun.
A producer arrives with
BBC Wales' third-best crack pipe
In her sweaty mitt.
The pipe is slid under the cubicle door,
Huw takes grateful hold of it
And then − ignition, evaporation, inhalation, and
A numbing, formless bliss.
I think
Huw takes things hard.
All the loss of life and property.
And the crap sports results.
They get him down.

She experiences a sudden, unexpected pain.

I wanted to be a novelist

And it was fucking hard.

Because . . . I had absolutely fucking nothing to write about.

I did research to fill that lacuna.

I went out and looked at people.

I looked at a girl at Time Flies.

She looked like Heather Graham.

After a while she came up to me and said: I'm going now.

You'll have to find someone else to look at.

So I did.

Beat.

And it's fucking hard.

You say to someone.

This typically against a worktop in a kitchen.

This typically in Grangetown.

You say.

There's usually a moment.

You . . . take the condom from him.

Because it's so much more romantic that way;

When the chick slides it on.

Romantic and empowering.

And sexy.

And usually I'm looking pretty diseased

So usually he's pretty fucking relieved

About that thin protective membrane.

And while I'm biting away at the foil wrap,

I share what's on my mind.

I say, look, this isn't just for tonight. Not for me.

And he looks back, and smiles,

And is almost certain I'm going to swallow, and he says –

Baby, I know. I know.

It's not just for tonight, I go,

It's for my novel.

And he stops. Or stares. Or gapes.

It's for my novel, I tell him.
I've gotten drunk and taken drugs and
I've come back to yours and soon we will have
Messily casual sex and I have done all this
Simply in order to enrich
My writing.
And this is usually the point
At which I get chucked out on the street.
Very, very few guys can handle
That kind of commitment.

1   A Sort of Homecoming

Mary Ann Street, 2359.

Boy   Did you see that?
He gave me this look
And then looked away.
He's doing it again.
He's looking at me −
− and now he's looked away.
What's that for? What's it
Supposed to mean, uh?
Don't you −
− don't think for a second
You're going to get away
With what you've just done.
Jesus / Christ.

Mum / Love.

Boy   I can't let him
Get away with that, though,
Can I?

Mum I suppose not, no.

Boy   So what're we gonna
Do about it, Mum?

Mum Why don't we just
Get off home
And warm ourselves up,
Have a think about it then.
What d'you reckon?

The **Boy** *pulls away from her.*

Boy   Fuck right off.
You are not fuckin gettin me –

Mum No, I know, my love,
I wasn't trying to get you,
I just –

Boy   Be careful now, alright?

Mum I will.
I am.

Boy   I know what.
I know what we should do.
Do you know, Mum?

Mum *looks at him.*

Boy   Do you?

Mum You tell me, son.

Boy   Let's get them.
Let's kill them all.

Man   This is a message.
And part of a system of messages.

Boy   It's on the internet.
What gases you need,
Where you get them from.
Do you think we should kill them, Mum?

Mum If that's what you want.

Boy   It's what they deserve.

Woman   This message
Is a warning about danger.

Mum Yes, of course my love.
       You come home, and you and me,
       We'll – make a bomb, and –

Boy   – we'll kill them. Every fuckin
       Last one.

The **Boy** *looks at his* **Mum**.

       What? What's up now?

Mum Nothing.

Boy   Don't get funny.
       I'm just about coming home, now, so –

The **Boy** *experiences a sudden, unexpected pain.*

Man   This place is not a place of honour.
       No esteemed deed is commemorated here.
       Nothing valued is here.

Boy   I've been alright.
       There's been cats looking after me.
       They don't always wanna talk, but then
       One will wander by with a hello tail up
       So you say hello, and they decide
       You're a bit grubby and
       You need a bit of a clean.
       They give you a few licks and
       In return all they want is some strokes and smooths.
       And even that is fine, cause it's nice
       Smoothing cats.

And then the **Boy** *starts to cry.*

Woman   The danger is present in your time
         As it was in ours.

His **Mum** *tries to comfort him.*

He lets her.

Boy   Cats just –
       – expect us to be good to them.

Mum They're nice, aren't they?

Boy They're better than persons.
Persons are bastards.
They don't fuckin care.

Mum Perhaps you could have a / cat –

Boy / There was this dog
That came to see me today
And he came round with me
For hours and when it got
Really cold we sat and he
Was on my lap, and I was all
Curled up round him. And I was
A coat for him, and he was
A hot water bottle for me.
He stayed for hours.
I thought he was gonna
Stay with me forever.
But then he went.

Mum Cause he knew I was coming for you.

Man If this message is difficult to read,
Please replace the marker
With one of a longer-lasting material.

Mum He knew you were going home.

Boy *looks at her carefully.*

Boy If I do come home,
Can I watch my *Simpsons* tape?

Mum Of course you can, my love.

Boy And then we'll kill the bastards,
For leaving me wet, and cold
And on the street, and all alone,
And for not giving a shit
Whether I fuckin lived or died.

Mum Well that's not
Very nice, is it.

Boy   They won't mind.
Cause they would've all let me die.
That means, they don't mind
Whether persons
Live or die.

Woman   If this message
Is difficult to interpret
Please re-state it
In languages you understand.

Boy   (*shouting*)
I wish to inform you
That tonight you will be killed
With your familes.

Mum It's already late, isn't it.
So – maybe tonight we'll get you home.
Get you fed and get you watered,
Then get you washed, and get you dried.
I'll tuck you up in bed and
I'll sit with you
Till you've closed your eyes.
And we'll let the bastards live –
– shall we?

Man   We considered ourselves to be
A powerful culture.

Woman   Sending this message
Was important to us.

Boy   Alright then.

(*To everyone.*)

You can live.
I'll let you live. But –
– just for this one night.

Appendix

Scene 6, 'Here Comes Everybody', pages 68–71
in English translation

I've found somewhere to park
I've parked the fucking car
I've taken the cover off the stereo
I've dragged the bags to the door
I've found the bastard key
I've called the fucking lift
I've done all this
When I remember –
Fresh fucking basil.
I need fresh fucking basil for the pasta sauce.
Fine. Okay. No fucking problem –
– back to Tesco's for the third time today,
Back into the car
Back to the flat –
Fine.
I walk in
Expecting to find Hywel
Running round the place screaming and sobbing
But no.
The place is almost silent.
Just – the tiniest sound:
A voice,
From the bathroom.
I push open the door.
I step inside.
I see Hywel, standing in the shower
His eyes closed
His voice trying
And failing completely
To carry the tune of some kitsch-funk mid-seventies
    Donald Fagen song.
I go – what the fuck are you doing?
They're going to be here any second.
He turns to me.

Water running down
His admittedly still interesting body.
'Don't let the whole thing stress you out, love.
'There's no need for all this fuss.
'It's just a little supper we're planning, isn't it?
'It's fun we're supposed to be having, not bloody
    heart attacks.'
And he smiles at me.
And I can see he thinks he's helping me
By saying this.

She goes to speak.

Pulls back.

Then –

Later, and the Gordons
And tonic is flowing down nice and easy
And still no sign of his fucking friends.
I ask him,
Who's coming to this fucking thing, then?
He says
'Oh, you know – everyone.'

She experiences a sudden, unexpected pain.

Just – 'everyone' – like that, with a dismissive little
Wave of his hand.
Everyone.
And this without even looking up
From the detail work he is doing
With the knife, and the oil, and the flame.
Bastard.
Everyone's coming to our little flat, are they?
Everyone in the world?
Everyone . . . in Wales?
Or just everyone in Cardiff?
If it's everyone in the world, well,
I'd suggest we go out to eat at
One of the city's larger public houses,
Because this kitchen can feel quite cramped

With more than six people in it.
If everyone in Wales is coming,
We'll have to put some of them in the spare room,
And bring them into the kitchen in separate sittings.
But . . . if it's only everyone in Cardiff that's coming
I'll just pop over next door and fetch a couple of
    extra chairs
And I'm sure we'll cope fine.

Beat.

He stops what he's doing.
He gives up on the gentle caramelisation of onions.
He even turns off the gas.
No, because I'm really looking forward to meeting
All your friends from Ely, Hywel.
And I can't wait to welcome the biggest
Somali community outside Africa into our home.
I've heard about something really interesting you
    can do
By mixing that chewing tobacco they're so fond of
With pure powdered ketamine.
I know a guy who says he can get me
The special K for quite a reasonable price
So now I just need a couple of Somali boys to sort
    me out
With the baccy and I'm off on a new kind of trip
    entirely −
− and at last
He turns round.
He peers at me for a second
Then, in a voice that isn't quite small
But is fairly quiet, he says
'We'll go out with your friends
'Next week. Alright?'

Printed in the USA
CPSIA information can be obtained
at www.ICGtesting.com
LVHW041100171024
794057LV00001B/181

9 780413 774378